OVERBOARD

ALSO BY BETH ANDERSON:

The Habitable World (Instance Press, 2001)
The Impending Collision (rem•press, 1997)

OVERBOARD

Beth Anderson

BURNING DECK, PROVIDENCE, 2004

ACKNOWLEDGMENTS:

Versions of poems in this volume appeared in *Apparatur, Barrow Street, canwehaveourballback?, Compost, Five Fingers Review, Greatest Hits: Twelve Years of Poetry from Compost Magazine* (Zephyr Press), *New American Writing, The Poetry Project Newsletter, Tarpaulin Sky, 26,* and *The Best American Poetry 2003* (ed. Yusef Komunyakaa, Scribner). "Hazard" was first published as a "Germ Folio" by Poetic Research Bureau in 2002..

Burning Deck Press is the Literature Program of ANYART: CONTEMPORARY ARTS CENTER, a tax-exempt (501c3), non-profit organization.

Cover by Keith Waldrop

OVERBOARD

Contents

You must be the visceral river.

You must think a little give

leads to affinities: the arrow

resembles the bird it will fly into.

—Alice Fulton, "Echo Location"

A Look and a Voice

The tale begins in a small desert town. As you divide things it becomes clear
that you must discard along the way. That's not philosophy, just a taste for straight
edges. And history of taste originates in a list checked off in steam on the mirror.
A: break and reconstruct, B: ledges to fall from, C: doorbells rung but ignored.
Start with B and who gets to keep the wreckage left once others have claimed
and sifted. The person who is most distraught will be allowed to hold my hand

once it is found and to give a speech about the goals and all at which I aimed.
There's no text amidst the bits of shattered talk. What are we using our voices for?
I can see even without a flashlight that one side of memory tells bright lies
to the other, pleasing all visitors who are ready for pleasure. Disconsolate, we break
ourselves into categories and shuffle well-wishers into corresponding piles.
Without fear the noon sun took up its collection, but now aches with its difficult

search for devotees. The face it has been given on paper does not resemble the face
it makes. When I revise it using the tools of triplicate with which I keep myself intact
leaves drop discordantly, components of table and season hit sidewalks in places
they cannot hold. For weeks there has been no rain, and gnats spin around the trash
seasonal indicators have become. Dust on our house mimics condensation on the oven door
and walls will not wear without the pressure weather provides. To pass time we hunt

for letters lending themselves to translation. With awkward shuffle on the sanded floor
I learn their stories by sorting them by touch, blindly as if for my ring of keys.
Something always is waiting to be found, a seat to be taken. On the flip side I feel
dressed with one sleeve on. Like flatware, we all have an address, a drawer, a noun
to which we like to be compared. Interruption reveals how distance shifts and falls in real
time and makes you a marker just like a subway sign. So determinedly there, in line.

The sacred ibis may be extinct, one of many reports
I hear but can't confirm. My chatter is meant to distract
you from my ignorance. Like bleeding, the facts
will stop moving but will not go away. But everything's fine;
don't be fooled by my infirm handshake. We may have to
jump turnstiles in our quest for the stolen arm of gold
but laws aren't worth as much as lore. Billboards and
oversized neon signs fill the sky in a form scorned as litter
but also supply that particular near-dark that feeds us.
Moving about in it are as many calls for action as
there are shadows on our windowpanes. Success collects
its prepositions from architecture, and we collect in turn
against future triumph. Beneath grave faces are claims
made regarding what I built for you and what you
tore down in response. A reciprocal relationship,
like those of mantises or other cannibals. I've inherited
a profession that sheds on the furniture and speaks
without listening to itself. Every second year
the theme is meaning; the alternates explore futility.
Cardboard guides left over when packing tape is gone
form figure-eights in the recycling bin. We have
been transitory long enough to forget how much attention
arranging demands, to erase the tenacious ribbons of grit
flush along walls where bookcases lean. Life springs
from objects or at least their observation. No matter
how many methods I use to recount my story—wrap
it around a misleap of narrative that fell on the car,
speak shivering with adrenaline—the audience still finds
greater satisfaction in shifting figurines. A dead cricket
has the potential to achieve greatness in this format
but in the here-and-now it is just a conquered pest,

evidence of earlier tales of woe and tentative conclusions.
The poison is in fact marvelous. Well, this too will
turn out to be an era, of clean streets for instance, or
temerity in the face of magnolia clones and literary taste.
The setting: warm, but not beach weather, and laden
with concrete. Also note that for once there is a correct answer.
We can expect to see quality art and hear adequate music. Get
a lift uptown. Give up our seats to people who need them.

The semblance of authority weighs as much as real clout,
tricking things we consume into dragging themselves up
from lovelorn rocks to take their places on our table.

I wished for a lady on a platter, not embossed but rather
a companion with hands beslimed with weeds and sea
and bound by chains most salient. Free will was thrown

out of context. Why else would *rescue* be murmured
countrywide but flood this vicinity, speaking to us
with fluently recycled arch words and handshakes?

Monsters that best vast armies of men are just one category
in which to collect. I remember things submerged in tidepools
by names that ring like yours. Irons link me to nostalgia

for freezeframe, for times before my landscape was littered.
Will the sacrifice of a photograph of life as we imagined it
produce the necessary remains? Internal bleeding reveals itself

as tenderness, then in patterns under the skin. I hadn't your bond
to flowerbeds at my fingertips, that's how much more
I rely on resuscitation than on lists of things to do.

The burden of the gaze pulls one arm away from and
the other into statuedom. A slow description may force them
to disembark from their lilypads. One drawback of being royal,

deportment's reek reflected in the blade of a well-used sword.
The blush held by your glass is filmic, a headache about
to become certain. How eloquently your face withstands

the general pressure to compare you to something inanimate.
By absorbing advice from the wind and like forces,
from stern crowds lingering on the cliffs, I will prove that

four syllables can force barnacles to open. When, after all,
is a beast not hungry. And so are we, jostling for speculation
as to who will wear the belt of three stars and whose waist

it last embraced. With too many wounds between its layered
scales, ownership has become ever-startled, comprising
a series of moments undoing the heroism they purport to praise.

Recording days by shutting off night
scraping away leaves to find the ground
our reliable narrator fares badly. A throat

with new skin glistening recites
memorials found on benches around town
but none entice. Rather find for me

a coincidence, a happenstance, someone
to run into on the street corner.
Make plans but not yet and in turn

I will serenade you from atop
an unfinished wall. Looking down
transforms bricks into letters of the alphabet.

It isn't the vantage point I'd choose—
my own framework is worldly
with leanings toward closure. We may deserve

nothing like what we've got
or turn out to be worthy of our consequential
groping toward a future of desserts.

Pollsters came round to undo the logic
of which we took possession
just after a motorcycle hit the hydrant in front

and a cat died inside. Feet of snow
would fall two winters later
portended perhaps by these

but maybe by other accidents
unremarked. Shade befuddles the breeze
stilling it with the regular turns

of a crank moving bricks toward a
wall in process. Precision
we want resides in frozen roots

and stages of frostbite collect there
like built-in bookcases spied
through open windows. I covet these

and covet a plot—all dirt, all potential,
a grime we'd proudly claim. Dead crocuses
are so thin as to be gestures.

Conditions of each fragment of cosmos
cannot help but inspire both remorse
and pleasure. I wipe sweat from a virtual brow

and find that something somewhere
deserves to be completely understood.
We turn out to intersect in stillest air.

A last chance dangles from your ceiling like mistletoe,
tests doubt in a grateful mirror. Burdened by sentiment or will,
all forms live internally. When fish are set loose from a net
a world flips over, lands in the midst of canals dug between centuries,

and takes up partnership in the most dangerous field.
Death stops by daily to greet those on the sea. Delve and drown,
with who knows how many more uncounted. Twelve,
twenty-four, eighty-two may be vast underestimates

for so many countries keep imprecise records. In them
we locate blueprints for drainage, irrigation, the breeding of plants.
Our own dropped breakables contribute to a method
rumored to erase utility, handed down in the form of crochet-trimmed towels.

I dry each filet by wrapping it in paper so no fluid remains
to splatter from the pan. In other media, questions are asked constantly
that attempt to evoke unspeakable names
but no one seems to want to know where power comes from until it goes off.

And only occasionally does water beg the question of source
in shorthand meaning *cruel, svelte, ready for skinning.* Can you teach me?
Or is it simply inherent or absent? Right or left handed, matter of course.
Hovels of headache and torn coat linings

form a genteel geometry adrift in its own mazelike reflection
and influence flails in the manner of final words
spoken from the floor long before you were found there.
I would prefer to avoid crescendo in these cacophonous times

inundated with mess. Try to subdue rash glances so stamps will go up
and crime reports can be filed. Dig into density to place well-wishes
and pull out a bone that later we'll sketch.
Only a half-truth can effectively soothe the shore. I'll strive to avoid

appearing aloof and promise to put as much charisma into *maybe* and *yes*
as I can muster. I now see where everything I will ever need is kept.

Hearsay Sonnets

From here we go there, from there I can't tell where we are.
It smells like exhaust despite the nearby sea. Who
is to say if remaining in check is worth anything, but
that phrase is certainly worthy of more. I tried to twist it around
and it tried to do to me what I had done to it. So we kept moving
and twisting and formed an inheritance, visible on the map
when we managed at last to hold it upright. Clarity
made everything around it better. Our chosen discipline shares
its name with a formula involving time and solace. One flash
is a sign of shore, two of tedium waiting humidly inland. I watch
for the tiebreak, coins flipped and scattered across my desk.
It's not that far south, this part of the shore, but birds and
debris compensate for missing miles. It's like living
among redwoods but without grandeur, just that *possible* air.

A teasing front hovers north. Like jumprope, you need
to know when to run in order to get through. This is
a formality we want to establish rather than break down.
Nothing implicated, just evidence that collecting happened
but you won't stay and then I will have left my heart
available for nudging. Worlds of lineage, pulling a line
together from all this text that we'll hook onto our orbit,
throw out of the maelstrom. The local who became a judge
is still sitting. We in contrast lease everything. This
plate is not mine. We rent the lawn and mower by the hour
and drive them to the right place at a time that could not
be refused. We hear palpitations underlying the race, move
together but don't sing the same way. We stretch carefully
before we work and gradually, like plants finding light.

With amazing speed the hills dried out until they were
so decimated that they disappeared. We searched for them
down wide industrial streets others could not believe
we'd survived when later we told stories of our hunting.
But I most want to turn somersaults in winter. I know I'll
forget the language that lives in my building, and this
disconcerts more than the act of departure. Severe stretches
will save the long tendons connecting each finger to a
skyline blip, stop a stack of cards from sliding to your lap.
I habitually conquer all my fears but only in my head
so that when faced with danger I can only freeze or flee.
We are not sorry to have this time together, to count lanes
fanning out from our position in a vast pattern of hoods
and roofs and impatience that might never move again.

Our weekdays folded into one temporal unit, costing us our
ordered lives. A price more than fair for respite from knocks
and rings and clinging to poles like carousel riders. You'll
never be a person who hates to walk, and I'll always near fatigue
before your step slows, but still we seem to need ourselves in
these incongruent forms. A blue bowl shows off yellow apples,
unripe greengage plums, the main intersection of town.
Please save me from cabbage roses with other versions of
domestic bliss. No longer will we decide where to stay based
on chances to participate in pastoral tableaux. Down the street
walnut trees grow and their ink stains the sidewalks with
an imprecise course of hopscotch. I'd hoped for artifacts but
found instead this tournament. We'll walk in the squares,
speak in shorthand, make rain with how much time we take.

There was silence when I put the receiver to my ear. This
is a place where people don't stop if a clear road's ahead.
Can territory alongside it continue to be shell-shocked
without the vote of tourism? They made all that land public
then let it burn down. Tight string cuts off the memory
it was meant to brace. I'll use it to tie up cornice and trim
under preservation rubric, for instead of practicing
we protected. We'll be ready if society comes by later after
making use of stored-up interjections. We've already refused
junk mail, forced politicians to come to the door and face us.
Passersby are watching clouds move in from the ocean,
comparing ancestors and contrasting main streets.
When the lights come up a true miscellany is revealed.
We are the only characters who give ourselves away.

Once inside I turned to you and began to describe the gate, what
made it, who oils its joints. How else would we see ourselves
now that your mirror is absolved from reflection and the moon
matters not. Fruit flies hover, slow enough to swat, swelling
as night falls. Old language and your arrival entwined
to make a text, overtaking what counted as ancient before dusk.
Nodding at the permanent residents is one kind of addition.
We count ourselves among the items on deck. All of them
keep coming at us daily and without remorse. What serves
as groundwork is the very pale green of leaves when light
passes through them, nearly yellow when lamps are lit.
Betrothals litter the dunes. Their tempers might be improved
by a near-deathly swim. The hottest day of the year has been
used as an excuse to tear off buds before they can bloom.

On the next page is another artist, or sometimes the same brush
and palette losing ground to early work. A treacherous slope
defeats rage then succumbs to loyalty. Renouncing steps for dirt
we keep climbing. All great cities have bad nicknames and
their own flexible landing gear. This plant flowers red, as
it did last year and the year before, but has done so late
to coincide with gravity. Seems we grow only when
we get enough to eat. Storms without precedent have used up
a list of names meant to see the century out, and everything
everywhere is saturated and splintered. Don't reach out the window.
Ignore what I said earlier about grabbing the golden apple.
Try instead to make your way to the capital without the aid
of pesticides. Every weekend I leave early to test my brakes
against forces holding limestone up, my neck bent into my back.

My feet hurt but not my sentences. I want this bug out
of my eye and banish it by turning it into a hairline fracture
waiting to happen. When the shore isn't yours anymore,
where the bay becomes the ocean and saltwater taffy is named
for associations rather than minerals, there we will embrace
rust and all things iron. Instead of sand, we will make of
this variegated dust a habit. There I'll be, with the *instead of*
pronoun. So much texture is trapped outside the skyline
and inside machines that churn cement. It will be so hot that
nothing will not catch on fire. But the battles we channel
draw on common names and force insomnia to morph into
vertigo before heading for the suburbs. I shall stick to present
tensions, anticipate not a swim but a search for pure water
and liken this vantage point to the best of the b-side songs.

Advertisements decaying on flood barriers complement
the quiet street. In the back-lit house opposite, I can see
telltale mending motions, held steady by privacy's
devastating grip. Where temperatures are moderate
tempers moderate themselves, and nothing you can say
will convince me this is a temperate zone. But the more salt
the better it tastes. Break *acclimate* into its parts before
you decide to stay. Embedded houses overhang as if
they were themselves jagged and thus able to sustain
injury without any change to basic character. Once daily,
it's not worth the time it takes in the rain. And in fact
we are much further south than we thought ourselves to be.
We sense there is a universe here in which to participate.
Both can be said of most places without any sacrifice.

A Locked Room

It must be assumed that somebody is telling the truth—else there is no legitimate mystery, and, in fact, no story at all.

—John Dickson Carr, *The Three Coffins*

1.

Traps are underfoot on every path. He who set them is bound
to property, waits to see if jaws glinting in moonlight will leave traces
when they close. He passes three doors on his way to find songs of grief

with interchangeable words and will go back over his steps past them
until negligence finds another place to keep its keys. I listen—no sound—
see three chairs, one outside each door. Even so, the hall does not invite delay.
Another gas lamp flutters against the gravel path, reflected in steel teeth

so that pieces of light are cut out. Evidently he has left and not given
us the means to suspect him, but there is no ladder; how did he descend?
We need not risk crossing open sky if imagination alone will suffice.

2.

We know the restaurants at which she ate, which roads she takes to regret,
who passed her the note clenched in her fist. We know she is independent
because she is the heroine but not a servant. We know that her state

has been brought on by knowledge and a refusal to voice what she suspects.
I am not a hero, and I expect the assassin this evening. When secret
formulas were stolen and tied to the tracks nobody bothered to pretend
that they were without value. We predict that soon we will embrace

another medium and hope we will be able to access the notes
we have made in this one. I arise and prepare, perhaps to wait,
perhaps to doze with open eyes, with her gaze, so pale and perfumed.

3.

Enter a series of recollections. This frieze is the third and I am further
away from the panels here than I have been before. No scan
of the story is possible. If I could locate the rose I would twist it and find

a cache of anonymous silver sent by magpie at backroad speed.
Your current pace will take you from here but send you off track, to where
everything tastes foolish, like perfect nectarines ripened into fermentation.
One cannot casually build. Call when the life you find is less like mine.

If we all agree to move to one location we will congest it and feed
on every available site, become interlopers among the quests to solve
dark cottage interiors, empty out commentary, detect the verge too late.

4.

The registrar's narrative finds him across from her while voices crash
and drop onto the quilt, undamaged. He lives like a wolf, with the hunter's eye
upon him, in an apartment surrounded by cement that keeps knowledge interned.

Held fast, in secret, it squints and grows by sifting through mattress guts.
A steward offered vast sums of money that were refused and his eyeglasses
fell from the bridge of his nose before imagination could recover them. I
gently imply that madness will pass from belief through theory to the silent cavern

containing all that is not held true. He expresses no surprise at the scratched but
whole chicken bones littering the ground where dogs guard the entryway
for we both know they will choke if they break through to marrow.

5.

On the window ledge a vine is crushed as if by the weight of a person preparing to jump. But just three feet separate the mulch-covered ground from the sill, and any leap would involve, then, a desire to live.

The absence of trust is a turning point in our sense of what should happen to the words *I saw a man.* The strange dissociation of matter has become a balloon inflated with helium, floating over footsteps sinking profoundly as they progress toward betrayal. Ankles and cobblestones don't mix

so all claims ably resist corroboration. I prepare again to enter the garden under the pretense of looking for traces he might have left. But once inside I will in fact rely on dreams to unveil both guilt and happiness.

6.

We thought it was over but heard another ending. This year was doomed
but not for those we'd handpicked. Instead, arch builders led crowds
of people into the light and away from portraits. Somebody saw us and was

so pleased that she infected us with pleasure. Our shining faces reflect in
buffed tabletops free of dishes and decor, create their own crowded rooms.
My elbows balance on the edge of something, *a veil drawn, a face shrouded.*
Her garden's pathogens lose none of their strength by giving clues to the press.

As a result, interruptions become part of the inquiry's deliberate din
and move it through time. Stains beneath polish date from a case of hidden love
that has resurfaced as a gaudy title. A kingdom falls, victim to aversion.

Columns interrupted my view and by moving to see one panel I would sacrifice
the rest. I watched the king despair in one alphabet of ever mastering another.
He is on the verge of losing his voice altogether after telling his beloved to speak.

Their invitation arrived on revolving doors and pulled to a stop outside my walls.
The burden of missing the same answer over again swamps me. I cannot revive
my interest, so fade. The fact that it is not a live performance drains me more.
That my nest is made of straw wrappers makes it harder. A critique

of rest draws jowls on fatigue itself. I never could get a sense of the whole
but still solved everything just in time in my bent silent head: see him dodge
while we, forsaken, are left behind to droop and doze in this overheated ruse.

8.

Deciphered, there are more instances of needing help than I can address
alone. Without confidence I agreed to plan a mysterious journey.
The call convinced me, with its determined attacks on claustrophobia

swinging from room to room and out the door like music run aground.
It perches on my desk and shreds paper into material for its collages
and steals my feathered pen. Enchanting evening, no stranger nearby.
All vistas remind them of being together and will until their minds see a

new part of the world and are able to erase evidence without sound.
The conductor announces a station torn asunder by wind then discarded,
as bereft of identification as a dress left crumpled on a bedroom floor.

We ate breakfast together in the sunlit room. Her soft voice denied any
involvement, but I knew I'd never comfortably sign any statement sporting
her word. Like the steps of blistering blocked shoes on dedicated toes,

her syntax returned to the point in every sentence, wore down one section
of sound-damped floorboards at a pace intended to clash with scenery.
Our words foliate these walls but eventually erode their own means of
support. Behind them, my goals hide even from me although we share

an office, nap nodding together in the afternoons. But danger beckons
and though I confess with some shame that I fear the blinking lights on
each skyline tower, in order to save birds of prey I will overcome myself.

10.

Now who remains in the room with me? With that question I lost control of all
I'd thought secure. Clad in remnants of an echoing gallery, the lady in black
left her voice behind to protect those who would walk under leaning ladders.

We took chances but never were able to find ourselves at home, instead
kept crossing borders and becoming visible. He escaped the fall
in a most unusual way. He sprang onto a wire fence just after the attack
and used grudges to keep his balance across the roof, break the pattern,

skip lightly atop the trap without triggering its jaws. I must loop a thread
around my wrist and carry my identity tucked in my sleeve instead of on it,
move past witnesses to take my place, wanting to whisper in every ear but silent.

In Passing

We look as though we have lived here all our lives
but only you understand the language in which we are addressed
by those who trust appearances. The years since you've climbed
those steps, taken that train, are many but are not obstacles to success.
There is an equally imposing number of broken statues in our
dreams and in our travels. In our memories they are whole. *Whole*
and *part* do not contradict on the internal timeline, where each
decade is marked off in increments as on a ruler, with room
between them for ideas as frozen as arthritic joints
to break off like marble arms. Burst in dry air like capillaries.

That was the year we met. Withstanding is a task assigned
to the third child of the third person to commit himself to memory.
At the time, the socket was jagged and we never believed it would
be anything but empty. Marks on our feet from sandal straps and sun
could be interpreted as death upside down and therefore
not necessarily dangerous. In delicious air we forgot
its foul pockets and made notes only where breathing was sweet and
locks were broken. Like the ridge on a ridgeback my hackles kept
arching until we reached the epitome of expatriate daydreams.
Instead of meaning *lovely hill town* our city of origin calls itself

by a moniker glazed with the leavings of industry. With a wet finger
I wrote a list of names in the grime on a wall. Something there
was waiting to be torn open. My understanding of how to manufacture
relies on rotator cuffs and heavy mallets. When the question of
particulars comes into play, I can answer which is the Roman name
and which the Greek, but you know when the next train leaves,
when the restaurants will reopen. And these practical matters
guide our lives away from lessons to other archaic indicators of status.
Obsession with the recovery of what has been taken from you
manifests itself as an excess of sleep. I have admitted that I cannot

tell interruption from metaphor and have been suitably reluctant to
look outside, at the possibilities beyond your life. An *instead*
is affixed to each view and every meal. All your blouses have
been laundered and lost and plots of land from which imagination might
learn have been covered with paper. What do they mean? Floating
around us and intending so much. Sending needles in cloth packets across
borders to the needy. Even the mice in the fireplace are attached to dark places.
At the foot of the steps I wait, eager to share my thoughts about kidnapping
and related legends but afraid to speak, to cut the abundance of words
that may hold invitations to us to become that which we resemble.

Their custom had been to straighten what others left askew.
They shared a spiraling bridge over busy roads
inviting thoughts of instantaneous travel, one like stone
the other like red soil, both on rivers. A specials board
or a sweat-soaked bench: either free to request an audience
with lost fidelity. At one foot, you feel as if
a tornado is chasing you, with tumbleweeds around and ahead.
On the other, you have just managed to catch the subway,
leapt onto the last, overheated car. Once you pass through
one story about gunfire and land in another about holdups
you start to accede that the guidebooks may be right. Crashes
and arson seal canes to hands in need and carve hobbles
out of honeycomb. The last day of winter has no chance
to come in time to this medium city where the north wind
was stillborn on the concrete capital. I read
the neighborhood's history in what occupants have scraped
into wet cement. Visit here, visit there. Even classrooms
now live in strip malls and recess can't get past meaning
how to lose your balance while losing a game.
Not until I caught the timesheet by its tip did you
agree to open your gift. I loosened my laces and retied them
slowly so I would not have to answer right away, for
the question was offensive, astute, and enticing all in one.

When the miracle happened, nobody reacted in the same way.
Variations in behavior could have been catalogued by someone industrious
but all with that trait were manifesting it elsewhere. Collecting, maybe,

or playing scales toward the improvement of other music.
I miss you, and don't mean to sound as if I don't
but all these occupations can distract even those who are at leisure

to choose what will happen next. Payments are made to
a general plan for how things go awry. Follow the car ahead
and end up in the wrong town or even tied to a phone pole waiting

for release, toes tagged with a name and time but no reason. We arranged
and undid our long-sought vacation, knowing how sleep eludes us
in the rooms of short-term rentals. It is possible to get away with

so slight a level of sharing. Much easier to march in pairs in song,
remember how people sound when recorded. One source of harmony,
regrets. And elusive, responsibilities stuck to the refrigerator door.

Save, for you cannot know when you'll change track and need scraps.
Delicate scrolls on the radiator sing a short cycle called *will this do?*
as the minimum contact forms in our rose bed, strides eastward after

slicing open the top of a convertible. I would offer assistance
but the familiar has stricken me still with scenery so clinical
that it plainly conveys how precarious everything beyond must be.

A postcard tells you a wild man has given away his piano.
While methodically pounding out a few basic tunes,
dictate a note to your memory: when a pen is found
please send an acknowledgement of receipt.
Meanwhile it's a relief to confirm blue skies over Reno.
Waiting to take steps that lead to departure
members of the crowd exchange vows at random.
So supportive of the blind spot, deliriously modern
until the desired one refuses your call
pushed by expertise and the ravings of certainty.
Letters flash systematically and break down
according to the shelf life of their innards
rather than their place in the phrase containing them
yet the results seem impossibly astute. In transit
you need quiet to see why it makes sense to be still.
We dream in order to learn what to do. Once awake,
we'll find a way out, dig a tunnel between
the first and fortieth days of agitation, burrow
into the tissue connecting seven wonders. The moon
must be waning for the spell to work properly.
In shadow a salt thief darts from step to net,
a cappella, but cannot help us find our version of escape.
We'll arrive where the hillside flattens out
and rings true only as a facet of comparison.
We won't imagine guidelines, for example, or
rampant moss. It's easier to conjure a stretch of sand
interrupted by nothing at all. Impulse has its advantages.
Witness its full house spread across the table and
which half of the torn wishbone remains in its hand.

It was a hard winter everywhere, and the angle at which difficulties found you
depended on how far away from the floodwall you were. When only a part of it
was built we drove to higher ground, a place from which to gauge the dimensions

of breadcrumbs floating on the river. It flooded halfway to where the hills roll,
approaching what had seemed hinterland. Ideally a region will release all citizens
who refuse to face rising water. With umbrellas hooked over arms and

placed in packs, they will seek and out all that has collected at the foot
of the temporary state of things. The impractical weight of every answer is
what makes any kind of flight a challenge. I consider and approach you

with an eye to appraisal, then panic when you flop the last three cards at once.
Please tell me that what we own remains accessible even if it means we must
shift as many tons of fluid as we have limbs. Dreams piped in open the elevator

and let other things through. Memories of music supercede hearing, splinter off
from rusting mesh, saturate discarded dolls, roil against the inevitable tires,
and lead you to the branch for which we long have searched. At last you will nap,

admit to fatigue, not just to sleep but the need for it. It was a hard winter
throughout the city. Its body was in shambles, and the wood paneling was soaked
then dried then froze. Are you spying on anyone these days? Relics of our visit

aren't old enough to take on the burden of meaning everything we are unable
to express in words. Accordingly, we organize ourselves around transitions
and move away from anything that might ask for a favor. Blink and you'll

miss something, but here's a second chance to sense it. Sit in the front of the boat,
where you'll be able to see anything visible but will also be drenched within minutes.
The photo of a double-hinged jaw and a person beside it to demonstrate size

can be found on postcards in any store near moving water. I have never caught a fish. Within the flood, debris floats, is suspended, and has sunk to rest on what is normally a surface. You may fall overboard but will remain, unavoidably, yourself.

HAZARD

Even as the dam is washed by the river

it adds to the river's bed. I skinned
my feet against it when resurfacing
to witness the slipstream rushing overhead

and engines visibly moving planes away.
To confirm that this, as every universe,

moves according to an intrinsic unplanned order
has taken hours. The structured conditions
don't lend themselves to formal display and

our escape should be arranged accordingly,
to exist simultaneously with chance. It

would be excessive to claim fluency but
both profiles appear to me visible alongside
their infamous vase and other forms that

cannot be forgotten once they have been seen.
Next the facts themselves will become clear

in vapor's dispersal or the speech
obliterated by its passing source, describing
nature as a set of constants refracted

by the masonry erected for its support.

An innate tenacity supports us so we can

invent the text from all angles at once.
A perfectly worthy subject for study was
under a veil and when removed

this veil turned to flame, early curricula
fell into ash. I want to involve myself

in your caprice. Our cab's interior might
recall downtown or just a loose iron grid
holding it there, holding us down.

Even as the dam is washed by the river
masonry erected for its support

will make *front* and *back* integral parts
of aspiration. The threat of pain
circulates in time with expectancy

and optimism. Grins dropped
into teacups, easily shattered, easily

and already stained. In some fashion I've
not yet ceased to regret, ideals sought
slide instead under the carpet and

may see red but will not recognize it.

There was not a knife in the dream

just my thumb independent of my hand.
And maybe this is the source of ownership,
a recollection of sharpness pressed

perhaps on hand and thus perhaps my own.
Otherworld substitutes for *substance*, for

deeper analysis, for bright red turning
through fence tines from leaf into flush
and blurring as speed increases.

An innate tenacity supports us and we can
see red but not recognize it. We call

forth *red* but abandon it for leaner history.
Appearing then disappearing alongside
the traveled road, place retains its prominence

and we march onward, uphill, establishing
factual context. We believe in something

dutiful, recompense with splintered ankles
every summit. By its own wing
the bird knows which twisting route to

follow. Its flight gives the bird itself.

I named our house after one country

then renamed it for another, creating a list
for the purposes of stinging trivia
where it lives. An integral part of certainty

is bleakness and its cohort, despair.
I will learn the names of elements

by turning away from fire and
locating the spent match. Possession
holds forth as befits nine tenths of the law.

There was no knife in my dream of
returning the bird to itself. Whether

spelled out or represented in digits
like fragments of collective imagination
gathering in the square, dice will roll.

Into anxious processes we cast them.
Effort is all we reckon could have withstood

pressure to build, to attend, to creep
underground. All transitions wind up here,
tapped out in code on window panes

their ashes blowing into the back seat.

Our escape will be arranged according

to where switches split. Whiling away
vindictive time, what other-handed
could I be, weighed down with iron ties.

I have taken over right-of-way
that did serve hunters estranged from quarry

and made this rail track into a secret route.
Despite an ambidextrous heritage
and dreams reliant on that source, still

I named our house after a country,
witnessed its ashes adorning the backyard.

Ahead of myself, though, in this practice
of identifying a skeleton by matching
its parts with ruts in the road. I hear tires

because of the rain. I hear rain
when it runs from the tires. Without place

the secrecy of our route cannot be
salvaged, for water has accumulated under
the porch and I have managed to lose

my grip simultaneously with chance.

II.

The address chosen as terra firma

for the first telegram turned out not
to be the first. Loss permeates the story's
texture. Over time it has been crushed

into a jagged state of indecision, part
of learning when to stop for water and

which signs to bypass. I scan second-hand
pages for patents and hope to evolve
away from memory tied into a cat's cradle

then raise two strings together, decline a third,
and am left with something flat after all.

Cycling through mazes, cutouts, perfectly
circular efforts of wind, we make the ribbon
untie itself. Bands of radar onscreen

attest to a given future, and their potential
captivates us, we who are unable to exist

without pins stuck on a map. Whose fingers
are whose, in which paper are we wrapped?
We threw all hats and thus created the ring

a place from which to sweep broken glass.

The grounds here house concern

tossed away like a penny that will not
bring luck to the thrower. I have bypassed
three coins, left them to be collected

by others. They shine with promise, shuttered
windows that line the street and could open

as we pass. Impressed by your foreshadowing
and calling cards, nerves cannot but pinch
and inspire reckless abandonment of dignity.

The address chosen on terra firma
resembles a place littered with broken glass

awaiting a broom. Ice retracts
from concrete and fills in the tread
of our shoes, shoring blood thinned

with aspirin and dreams of altitude. I won't
gamble on this petition, will instead confirm

each signature's validity. Sudden noise
sent images flying as from capture, distress
became property, foreshadowing posture

with a dignity dawning years too soon.

Adding plus *up* equals *idiom.* My ruler

resembles a pane of glass etched
with numbers and lines. I tried to measure
the girth of my investment with beakers

and lead weights, but none would adjust
to our briefcases or persons. Exchange

of one beaker for the ruler didn't help, but
one mark replaced another with ease.
That part of the collection should be read

in direct light. The grounds here house concern
with a dignity dawning years too soon

prematurely assigning *disbelief* a meaning
like that of *confusion.* Not missed
or missing, for subtraction has no sidekick.

Division has any number of prepositions
at its disposal. Words we speak in public

harbor interest in all sites laboring to replace
the field. Pull me out of this portmanteau
and add me on. Divide me up. Present me.

This project is doomed by its own locale.

Our view of risk renders it perilous

simple as sweat on a cold bottle left out.
It is equally clear that entire professions
can fit into a single petri dish

battle-ready but brittle and small.
Drooping cities betray one another

with rigorous mutual translation,
accomplished by writing numbers
in cardinal then ordinal form, proof

that *adding* plus *up* equals *idiom*.
This project is doomed by its locality

and its widowhood. Eavesdropping
has populated our inroads and sidewalks
with various defective snippets

read in transit, recorded as remembered
with shaking pen on paper scraps.

A webbed footprint made up of these
entangled errors is both primitive and
collectable, summing up my memory

of safe houses with its tender tread.

I lifted two shells together, left the third

until I could tuck the first beneath one arm
all to drain the mystery from chance.
Our conversation rejects other voices

will not contribute to the air but
breathes it greedily, then with caution.

Our steps have left traces like burnt rubber
on the landing outside, results of a grip
that is constant and lets go only once

imprinted. Risk renders itself perilous,
transforms safe houses with a tender tread.

Air brushes past and states intrusion
but the only noise is made by a passing bird
and its only trace is an echo

not contact of air and sleeve but that
of sleeve and arm, arm recalling.

Touch one shell to confirm at the risk
of extinguishing hope. Muddy prints
in a row before me lead over the side

of what has turned out to be flat after all.

III.

I must express grief though it is

coincidental to the broken object
at my feet. Opalescent shards catch
on brown paper like a journey shattered

into its legs. Until this accident
no inclines threatened to free my dreams

of explanation. I travel 52 weeks a year
to collect sightings of force and
watch my senses shape their own frame.

The final gesture of each vehicle affirms
how little I know of my own construction.

My route skirts around what *criminal*
means, soggy against the skyline
where river meets park and

the curvature of bridges mimics
denser inland tracks. Laundry furnishes

the air with new verticality, shirts like
flagstones, darkness the grit between them.
We climb their scarred surfaces to

no other world but this, our own creation.

The concealment of longing is the apex

of a room distinguished by quarantine,
its used air, its held breath.
These remnants of ambition

come to mind piece by piece as
the temperature drops. Abandonment

in this case is an act not of treachery
but of unrequited love. Timeless creatures
like fate and life are forced

to express their grief in this
and no other world. At first created

for long distance, a floating material
passion now exists solely to serve
regret. Not one of the region's

products will be sold or understood.
Before we learned to link art and devotion

the aluminum screen door seemed to us
a perfect expression. Like *thanks,*
which we speak so often

to guarantee ourselves the last word.

We tell ourselves that the story is all

there is available of truth. Circling
in a pattern of stops and starts,
proof is like a cord tied to the dock by

someone who cannot match knots with
their names. My grip may be addressed to

a banister, to the opposing wrist, my heart.
Internal trembling is not grief but
its expression, refused a means of utterance.

The concealment of longing also serves
to guarantee us the last word

perfect for gentle rolling hills and the even
pulse these feed. What they endanger
is the unspoken life, losing it and having it

equally. No allergies, no lust, no inexplicable
dreams. No veils and unveilings. It's a case

of not knowing what to do with lies
when we find them. Unable to elaborate
on suspicion, a threat that should be shouted

across courtyards stays inside, tethered.

However remote disaster may seem

and despite primary sources that
wring sorrow from deliberate tales
of grim emergency, those trapped

within the incident have responded
to coincidence, and their accounts

act together to generate urgency.
Counting on stimuli and temperament
always results in a prime number.

We tell ourselves that the story is all.
Despite courtyards we stay indoors, tethered

to a hallowed vision, a published article,
hope emergent. I wish to reconcile
denial with success, perhaps

with joy found in gleaming surfaces
and dusty carpets beaten. You can see

why a brim ideally should cast a partial
shadow, leave the rest of the face
beckoning to its readers with history

realized when information is withheld.

The final gesture each boat makes

as it leaves port is a salute to shore.
Halos appear and fade in accord
with paint tinted by harbor muck

and the point at which canals disappear
in their dedication to perspective.

Applying the solar scheme of things,
from boat to boat ceases to be a measure
that matters. To be a measure at all.

However remote disaster may seem, it can
be realized when information is withheld.

Quicksilver we've heard of, like small
fish swimming in time without
maps or words. Their relationship to water

is the closest thing we have found
in our search for parallels. What

fever does. Salt white streaks on
an ill-lit road. The foundations of this
neighborhood resting on vermin. That

I know so little of my own construction.

IV.

Discrepancy traces the flat world along

edges of the telescope's lens. We will not
pass as human design until humility
bows its head, for the climate suggested

by bold insight has become untenable. In tandem
with measured thought, we face ourselves

in the flourishes encircling a priceless
work of art. When our reflections initiate talk
of real life I realize mine has thus far been.

Age-oldness is now replenished,
pulling inward from its own flawed orbit.

Territory pivots as the painting is hung
on its side, positing position as the
result of needing to be recorded, by

cauldrons or plaster or enlisted to provide
expanse where none at first appears. A

spectrum reveals greater range within its
categories the longer we stay, resting,
framing elusive ideas with our hands and

a memory of cathedrals motioning skyward.

Between revolution and time is one

day, one axis balancing churchly impressions
with third rails. We each press into a
recess lining the tracks

to avoid trains, tourists, some versions of the planet.
Pleasure puts forward the sole movement herein

and the only sound results from a frame's
collapse. A quake may manifest collective
action but for all that is not divine.

Discrepancy traces the flat world
along a memory of cathedrals gesturing

skyward, likely to elongate lineage. Your
bearing does not let slip the means of suspension
or source of gold. We continue to circle

as if navigation could be achieved
with dreams and leaded glass. A braid

hangs loose, nearly straight, serving
like a ruler as one object of adulation.
That is missing from my portrait and every

image summoned from suspended belief.

The great solemnity of structure is no longer

light kept out but lights turned off. A work
on one wall faces another on the other,
the first a teacher's optimism sketched in

and stretched, linen-and-table-like.
Suspended over an inviting throne

speech is exchanged as positions rather
than words. None of the grandeur common
to an even surface involves itself with this

three-dimensional perspective. Between
revolution and time exists one image I can

summon from suspended belief, that inclined
planes have fuller names when creation
must account for its underpinnings, with

lists and rosters and cornerstones imprinted.
Envy offers a breakthrough to physicality,

its curvature mapped onto a flat sheet yet
understood as deep, shallow, staggered and
staggering. From geometry we borrow power

attribute uprising to 20/20 vision.

Instead of vowing, I will imagine pinnacles

and the stringent methods required
for their construction. Breakdown is based
in overextension, something Napoleonic

the object of my grasping hand. Frenetic
scheming will be required if our frontiers are

to be presented as they wish to be immortalized.
We miss open spaces because of the calm
we are told is embodied by their sprawl.

The great solemnity of structure no longer
attributes uprisings to those with 20/20 vision.

We realized this and took ourselves
in hand to view the trembling fields
more truly. But through our bedraggled blinds

forearms burdened with household debris,
we could see only according to records

inscribed on impermanent planes. What
would I have written later had I not
written then of the wine darkness

cribbed from another's vision of the sea.

Humanity's age-oldness is now replenished

where it was replaced. With all we have
come to expect from longevity comes too
this vision of a renewable resource.

Focus tossed to the four winds will seek
order in those currents, turn next to the

corners of the earth. In communities
uncommunal we keep missing the chance
to tie planetary dimensions to method.

Instead of vows, I will imagine pinnacles
cribbed from another's vision of the sea

some nautical verb enacted here
before us. Held in check with items plucked
from a list of theories gone wrong, our

primary option exploded and its
apparatus fell into deep water. Naturally

what we wish is to think ourselves serious
but according to the age of its firmaments
this must be a sun-centered universe, ever

pulling inward from its own flawed orbit.

This book was designed and computer typeset in 10 pt. Palatino with Phyllis initials by Rosmarie Waldrop. Printed on 55 lb. Writers' Natural (an acid-free paper), smyth-sewn and glued into paper covers by McNaughton & Gunn in Saline, Michigan. The cover is by Keith Waldrop. There are 1000 copies, of which 50 are numbered & signed.